CONT

Written by: Peter Elson
Design & Production: Vicky Andrews
Cover Design: Colin Harrison

Photographs:
Liverpool Post and Echo
Colin Lane, Gareth Jones, Jason Roberts,
Andrew Teebay, Gavin Trafford,
James Maloney and Tom McCarten
Mirrorpix
Library of Congress Archives Canada

With special thanks to Brian Johnston,
Liverpool Post & ECHO image archive

Contact us: lostliverpool@trinitymirror.com

Trinity Mirror Media

Managing Director: Ken Rogers
Senior Editor: Steve Hanrahan
Editor: Paul Dove
Senior Art Editor: Rick Cooke
Senior Marketing Executive: Claire Brown
Sales and Marketing Manager: Elizabeth Morgan
Sales and Marketing Assistant: Karen Cadman

Business Development Manager / Advertising
Will Beedles 0151 239 5949

Printed by Buxton Press
ISBN 9781908695482

OUR DARK LADY

By Peter Elson

THE River Mersey of our imagination is like so much in life, namely one of deceptive appearances.

The universal vision is one of a great swathe of heavy, dark water that is more sea-like than river, across which great ocean liners, bustling ferries and gargantuan tankers and container ships sail.

The backdrop is inevitably the Pier Head's 'Three Graces' always with the Royal Liver Building's twin clock towers prominent.

It is conjured up in popular culture with Merseybeat pop music, developed from the port's close links with North America and hence its music. The river achieved top-ten chart status in 1965 with Ferry Cross the Mersey, by Gerry and the Pacemakers (and in a film of that name). Two years later, the Liverpool Poets' The Mersey Sound compilation book made versifying as hip as it was in Lord Byron's heyday. Yet this is only part of the fuller picture. For the Mersey has more strikingly different guises than most waterways.

For a river of such magnificence in the public consciousness, the Mersey is rather like an aspirational showgirl of humble provincial origins determined to prove herself in the eyes of the world.

She enters into the world as the offspring of the Rivers Goyt and Tame coming together by a Stockport dual carriageway and shopping centre.

As with all such stories there is an alternate version which suggests that the River Etherow is also involved in the birth. The Mersey's name originates from the Anglo-Saxon words "maeres", meaning boundary (between the kingdoms of Mercia and Northumbria) and "ea", a river.

Even today, in the era of mass communication, this great border river still acts in this fashion: splitting opinions, separating physically and psychologically the counties of Lancashire and Cheshire, dividing the lifestyles of Liverpool and the Wirral.

Naturally, in her journey of 70 miles or so to her place as a Diva of the Deep, the Mersey has a mixture of fair flowing progress and set-backs. ➤

The Dutch schooner Oosterschelde
moored at Albert Dock in 2011,
contrasts with the modern city backdrop

Liverpool waterfront in the late 1940s, after wartime devastation. The Strand and Overhead Railway bisect this page north-south and the Goree Piazza and White Star Buildings burned out, lower centre; Clarence Dock power station only has two 'Ugly Sisters', top. The awnings of Exchange Railway Station dominate, upper right, and the burned-out Custom House is bottom right

➤ After a prosaic advancement through southern Manchester, the Mersey suffers the indignity of being diverted into the Manchester Ship Canal to maintain water levels with the River Irwell, but is freed at Rixton.

However, the real step-change is at Howley Weir, Warrington, below which the Mersey becomes tidal and starts to establish the image we know so well.

Like so many star performers, our river loses form at times and she bloats out while flowing past Fiddlers Ferry, only to retrieve her narrow waist through the Runcorn Gap.

Here, the famous Silver Jubilee road and Britannia (or Ethelfleda) railway bridges leap over the sandstone gap to join Runcorn and Widnes. Once there was a third crossing in the form of the Transporter Bridge and this could occur again with the Mersey Gateway road bridge.

Meantime, on the Runcorn side runs the river's trade usurper, the Manchester Ship Canal.

Then the Mersey turns northwards and broadens with the estuary spreading to its widest at a breath-taking three miles.

Viewed from Weston Point ridge on the southern side, the often silver-coated river seems like an inland ocean, entirely deserving the Hale Head Lighthouse (sadly now defunct).

Like many parts of the Mersey (especially since the Mersey Basin Campaign cleansing initiative), the estuary's mudflats are an important home of extensive wildlife. Indeed, further upstream at Fiddlers Ferry, famous for its power station, otters are now breeding at a new Site of Scientific Interest. Salmon have been seen jumping Howley Weir, Warrington. In 2009 the Mersey was declared to be one of the cleanest UK rivers.

As if the incentive of reaching the world famous city and port ahead, the Mersey starts to speed up from Ellesmere Port, once again narrowing, this time to about three quarters of a mile wide between Liverpool's Albert Dock and Birkenhead Woodside ferry terminal.

Just as the western Pennines bequeathed us the Mersey, so Liverpool is the gift of the Mersey. By happy coincidence of geography, it not only superceded, but also long out-lasted other once dominant west coast ports such as Chester, Lancaster and Whitehaven.

The key reason is deep water. As the river is forced between the unyielding Liverpool and ➤

➤ Wirral sandstone banks it can achieve a speed of up to six knots. The tidal range runs from 13.4ft at neap tide to 32.8ft at spring tide – a difference second only to the River Severn in the UK.

That was not helpful to the Benedictine monks of Birkenhead Priory who were granted ferry rights by King Edward II in 1318 and a crossing could take 90 minutes (if you were lucky).

But in modern terms this deep water means the world's largest cruise liners can berth in the heart of the city at the new Liverpool Cruise Terminal, close to the Pier Head, just as they have done for more than a century.

Probably the most celebrated sight in recent years has been the presence of the world's biggest ocean liner, RMS Queen Mary 2, flagship of Cunard Line (founded in Liverpool in 1840), at this city centre mooring.

Just as importantly, giant tankers can reach Tranmere Oil Terminal, to supply the Ellesmere Port, Stanlow and Weston Point petro-chemical complexes.

The American author Herman Melville hailed Liverpool Docks as being a construction on a par with the Pyramids. Walter Dixon Scott said they were a "seven mile sequence of granite-lipped lagoons".

They constituted the most advanced port system in the world, interconnected by lock gates enabling ship movements 24 hours a day irrespective of Mersey tides.

Visionary thinking also meant the Gladstone Lock into the Gladstone Docks was built in excess of the Panama Canal dimensions, a decisive factor then, as now, in ship size. Large container ships can still access the Liverpool Docks system (much of which is technically in Bootle) including the 1972 Seaforth Dock container terminal.

However, to keep up with worldwide trading advances, dock owner Peel Ports Mersey is building a Post-Panamax berth in the river to take the new generation of super-size container ships, following the widening of the Panama Canal.

As the Mersey's water spill into the Irish Sea and mix with those of the Atlantic Ocean, welcoming Atlantic grey seals, bottlenose dolphins and harbour porpoises, it has been an exceptional journey.

But while the Pennine rain falls and the water flows, this is a journey that never ends, and the river remains as important now as it ever has been to our well-being.

LIVERPOOL
AS IT APPEARED IN 1650.

1 The Battery.
2 Old Church.
3 The Tower.
4 Custom House.
5 Water Street.
6 Town Hall.
7 Beacon Everton.

8 James Street.
9 Old Castle.
10 Pool Lane.
11 Low Hill.
12 Townsend Bridge
13 The Pool.
14 Road to the Park

Ships riding at anchor in the Mersey of 1836, the year of severe storms, when several vessels met their fate in the river

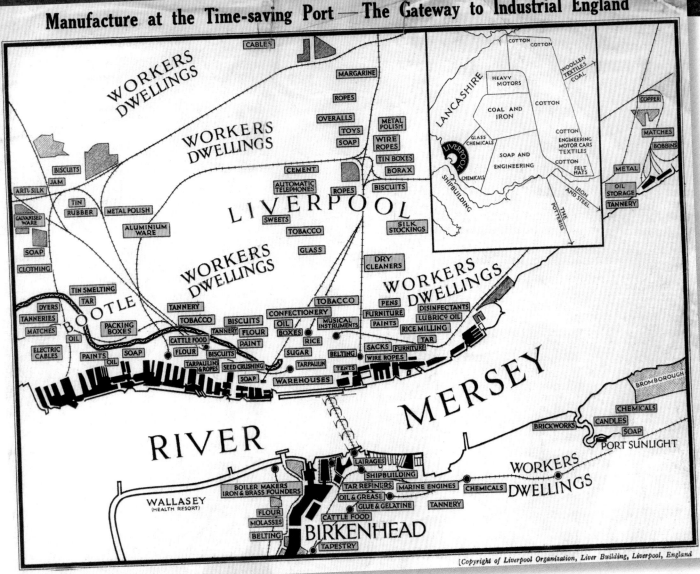

Manufacture at the Time-saving Port — The Gateway to Industrial England

WORKERS DWELLINGS

WORKERS DWELLINGS

CABLES

MARGARINE

ROPES

OVERALLS

TOYS

SOAP

METAL POLISH

WIRE ROPES

TIN BOXES

BORAX

CEMENT

BISCUITS

JAM

ART. SILK

TIN RUBBER

METAL POLISH

GALVANISED WARE

ALUMINIUM WARE

AUTOMATIC TELEPHONES

ROPES

BISCUITS

SWEETS

TOBACCO

SILK STOCKINGS

GLASS

SOAP

CLOTHING

WORKERS DWELLINGS

DRY CLEANERS

LIVERPOOL

WORKERS DWELLINGS

TIN SMELTING

TAR

DYERS

TANNERIES

MATCHES

OIL

ELECTRIC CABLES

PAINTS

OIL

SOAP

BOOTLE

PACKING BOXES

TANNERY

TOBACCO

BISCUITS

TANNERY

FLOUR

CATTLE FOOD

FLOUR

BISCUITS

PAINT

TARPAULIN & ROPES

SEED CRUSHING

SOAP

CONFECTIONERY

OIL BOXES

RICE

SUGAR

TARPAULIN

WAREHOUSES

MUSICAL INSTRUMENTS

TOBACCO

PENS

FURNITURE

PAINTS

BELTING

SACKS

WIRE ROPES

TENTS

WORKERS DWELLINGS

DISINFECTANTS

LUBRIC9 OIL

RICE MILLING

TAR

FURNITURE

RIVER

WALLASEY
(HEALTH RESORT)

LAIRAGES

SHIPBUILDING

BOILER MAKERS IRON & BRASS FOUNDERS

TAR REFINERS

OIL & GREASE

GLUE & GELATINE

MARINE ENGINES

CHEMICALS

TANNERY

FLOUR

MOLASSES

BELTING

CATTLE FOOD

BIRKENHEAD

TAPESTRY

MERSEY

BROMBOROUGH

CHEMICALS

BRICKWORKS

CANDLES

SOAP

PORT SUNLIGHT

WORKERS DWELLINGS

LANCASHIRE

COTTON COTTON

HEAVY MOTORS

WOOLLEN TEXTILES COAL

COAL AND IRON

COTTON

GLASS CHEMICALS

COTTON ENGINEERING MOTOR CARS TEXTILES

SOAP AND ENGINEERING

COTTON

FELT HATS

LIVERPOOL SHIPBUILDING

CHEMICALS

IRON AND STEEL

THE POTTERIES

COPPER

MATCHES

BOBBINS

METAL

OIL STORAGE

TANNERY

Gladstone Dock under construction, May 1927

STAR PERFORMERS

Above, men of the company of HMS Starling with the remains of two U-boats destroyed in the Battle of the Atlantic, 1944. Right, Winston Churchill speaks to men of the Merchant Navy in this Liverpool dock shed, commending them on their work – April 29, 1941. Below, a German midget sub is towed through Birkenhead in the Naval Thanksgiving Week on September 22, 1945

A steam caisson is placed across the entrance of Sandon Dock in November 1929, so the lock gates can be repaired

ROYAL PROGRESS

The 38,000-ton RMS Windsor Castle, the new Union-Castle Line flagship and the largest liner built in England, makes a majestic Mersey debut from her fitting-out basin at Cammell Laird's to Gladstone Dock, in May 1960, to have her rudder fitted. On her maiden voyage to Cape Town and Durban it is said that every First Class passenger was titled. She was Union-Castle's last express South African mail boat and withdrawn in September, 1977

CRATE EXPECTATIONS

Above, dockers at work moving cargo in 1965, and left, fruit cargo in a docklands warehouse

Top, the 29,000 ton bulk carrier Star Acadia is launched at Cammell Laird, September 1969. Bottom, aerial photograph of Seaforth from the 1960s, demonstrating how the town indeed marches forth towards the sea

HEAVY SMOKERS

Alexandra tugs belch fumes as they pivot
Cunard liner RMS Ascania away from
Princes Landing Stage (bound for Quebec
and Montreal) before an audience on the
stern of Elder Dempster Line's Apapa, about
to leave for West Africa, on October 7, 1954

One of Aznar Line's express fruit cargo liners, famous for their 'Banana Boat' cruises to the Canaries, enters Gladstone Lock in August, 1975

GATEWAY TO THE WORLD

CANADA BOUND

Left, leaving Liverpool for Canada, 1925.
Right, Canadian military personnel en route to Canada cover every inch of the foredeck, including the derricks, on board RMS Mauretania, Gladstone Dock, December 1945

Library of Congress Archives Canada

Cunard Line's RMS Campania of 1893 leaves Princes Landing Stage, with the company tug tender Skirmisher alongside. She took the Blue Riband of the Atlantic from the Inman Liners, but was superceded herself by Lusitania and Mauretania in 1907
Library of Congress Archives Canada

One of Inman Line's beautiful three-funnelled Blue Riband Transatlantic speed queens, either City of Paris or City of New York, being tendered off Princes Landing Stage in 1900
American Stereoscopic Company / Library of Congress Archives Canada

PROMENADERS

Stylish Edwardian ladies stroll along George's Landing Stage in 1901. Left, emigrant passengers pose for their photo on the promenade deck of Cunard White Star's MV Georgic, prior to leaving Liverpool for Australia on April 8, 1949

Most people used Liverpool as a transit station to other parts of the world, but many who arrived in the city en-route to the Americas or Antipodes, never made it any further than Aigburth or Anfield. Others made their home in Liverpool after coming here as sailors, creating the oldest Chinatown in Europe, for example. Above, a view of Pitt Street, the famous road that formed the hub of the Chinese community in Liverpool

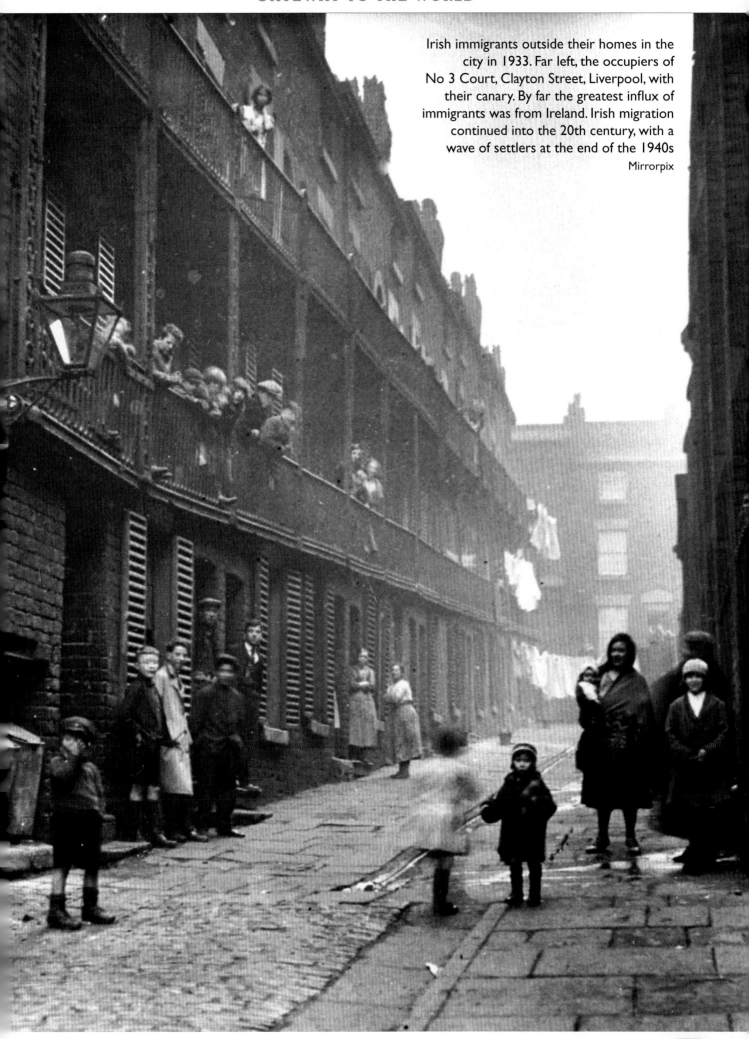

Irish immigrants outside their homes in the city in 1933. Far left, the occupiers of No 3 Court, Clayton Street, Liverpool, with their canary. By far the greatest influx of immigrants was from Ireland. Irish migration continued into the 20th century, with a wave of settlers at the end of the 1940s

Mirrorpix

MERSEY MONARCHS

Main picture, Canadian Pacific's new flagship, Empress of Canada, seen here leaving the River Mersey and passing Perch Rock lighthouse, New Brighton, en route for Quebec and Montreal on her maiden voyage, April 27, 1961.

Left, first class passengers board Alexandra's tug tender Flying Breeze to reach a liner anchored mid-river on June 23, 1950. Ahead lies Isle of Man Steam packet Company's King Orry.

Right, Canadian Pacific's Duchess of Bedford prepares to leave Princes Landing Stage on her maiden voyage on June 1, 1928

Canadian Pacific's fabulous flagship RMS Empress of Britain, circa 1936, when commanded by Victoria Cross holder Commodore Ronald Neil Stuart, VC, DSO, RD, RNR, of Toxteth, Liverpool, and Liverpool College old boy

Empress of England arrives in the Mersey from Canada and makes an impressive spectacle for holiday-makers at New Brighton, May 1958

The dock board crane Mammoth lifting the 76-ton stern funnel casing off Mauretania at Gladstone Dock, where the giant Cunarder was undergoing an extensive refit in September, 1946, after wartime trooping. Frames for canvas awnings needed in the tropics are still in place, which won't be needed on the North Atlantic

NEWLY MINTED

Mauretania on her way down the Mersey to Gladstone Dry Dock, to have her rudder fitted, passing the Clarence Dock power station, May 15, 1939

Already with her funnels painted in wartime black, time is fast
running out for Liverpool's pride, RMS Lusitania of Cunard Line,
shown in 1915, just before she was torpedoed and sunk by
Germany's U-20 on May 7, that year, with the loss of 1,198 people
Library of Congress Archives Canada

Cunard Line's secondary services were provided by the likes
of RMS Saxonia, circa 1900, a classic Edwardian steamer with
low superstructure, four masts and a ridiculously tall funnel
Library of Congress Archives Canada

ALL WHITE NOW

After closing Cunard's Liverpool – New York service in 1966, RMS Sylvania was repainted white for cruising and revived the line's first cruises from Liverpool since the war. Here she has her winter overhaul in Gladstone Graving Dock, including a change of propellors. The stern anchor was an emergency measure for sailing in the confined St Lawrence River, Canada

ARK AT THIS

A Cock tug belches smoke as it tows Ark Royal into Cammell Laird's wet basin for fitting out immediately after launch by the Queen Mother on May 3, 1950

Cunard's RMS Carinthia backs off the landing stage aided by Alexandra tugs, at the start of a sailing to Quebec and Montreal in a view from Canadian Pacific's Empress of France, on February 2, 1957, by Walter McEvoy

Cunard flagship QE2 on her first visit to the River Mersey, July 24, 1990, to mark the 150th anniversary of the company's founding in Liverpool

Partly framed by the prow of the Liberian-President Tubman's yacht, the cable-laying ship Mercury, is towed into the fitting-out basin at Cammell Laird's in Birkenhead, July 21, 1962

31

DOCK LIFE

SAW DOCTOR

A carpenter lights his pipe at Gladstone Graving Dock, November 1962, with Empress of Canada under repair. Right, machine parts are loaded in, January 1968. Bottom, the Royal Liver Building is overshadowed as the camera sees it by the 40-ton, 90-foot long tank trundling to the Herculaneum Dock en route to an oil plant in Venezuela

ALL CHANGE

Above, Waterloo Docks. Right, the times they are a changin' as British & Irish Line's rapidly increasing container traffic in February, 1971, spills over from Princes Dock, in Liverpool, and the company prepares to move to its new Wellington Dock complex. The fine waterfront warehouses have gone, but at least the best – Waterloo Warehouse, left, is now converted to apartments

GULL'S VIEW

A tranquil mid-1960s aerial shot of the docks immediately north of the Royal Liver Building. A Manx car ferry lies off the landing stage and Clarence Dock power station's three 'Ugly Sisters' quietly fume

SOUTH DOCKS

Above, Coburg Dock, with a fine
collection of Dock Board dredgers
and the Isle of Man Steam Packet
cargo ship, Peveril, right.
Right, Garston Docks, well-
equipped to handle bulky timber
baulks, March 1960

DOWN SOUTH

Left, South docks, showing Canning
Dock, Albert Dock, Salthouse
Dock, Wapping Dock and Queens
Dock, 1981, by now deserted

Albert Dock office, 1960.
Above, aerial view of the
Albert Dock, August 17,
1980, in a sea of mud

ROYAL REOPENING

Prince of Wales unveils the commemorative plaque in the restored Albert Dock, May 24, 1988. Below left, submarine HMS Saga on public view during Thanksgiving Week at the Naval Exhibition in Canning Dock, September, 1945. Right, a postcard of Canning Dock sums up the city's past with the Royal Liver Building in the background

Canning Dock, Liverpool

Birkenhead 1973, still busy with traditional
cargo ships belonging to Lamport & Holt,
Palm, Henderson, Blue Funnel and Clan Lines

The BP tanker British Ensign being launched at Birkenhead, October 4, 1963

Right, a view of the deck cargo of the Empire Byng, lying in the West Float, Birkenhead, showing 16 railway coaches, part of a total of 29, she is carrying to South Africa, January 1949. Bottom right, Vittoria Dock, packed with pipes and train wheels

WORK
AND
PLAY

NEW BIRTH

The newly-launched Isle of Man steamer Mona's Isle at Birkenhead. The ship is towed by Thistle Cock into the Wet Basin as crowds gather round to watch, October 1951. Mona's Isle was built to such a high standard by Cammell Laird, she was nicknamed 'The Yacht' by her Steam Packet crews

THISTLE COCK

OH BUOY!

Some of the Mersey's huge marker buoys being repaired in the Buoy Store at Herculaneum Dock in 1951. Right, the changeover of the familiar funnel company colours – Rea's distinctive black diamond is painted over the Furness red and black as the three tugs have their colours changed in a Birkenhead dry dock, 1969. Below, the crew of the Empress of France sign on in August 1959

Above, a misty day at Four Bridges in Birkenhead dockland, December 21, 1935. Bottom, buses climb the steep hill from Birkenhead Woodside Ferry, at the beginning of the evening rush period as the clock on the Royal Liver Building across the Mersey chimes five o'clock, April 23, 1962

GIG GUYS

Ray Gilland and Derrick Banks, at work in their gig boat Jaguar at Gladstone Dock, November 1971, taking the lines from Blue Funnel's Eumaeus

LIFELINE

New Type 42 destroyer HMS Campbeltown comes out from under wraps at Cammell Laird in August 1987. The £70m warship was dubbed 'The Lifeboat', because, without the order from the then Defence Minister Michael Heseltine, the yard would not have survived

Shrimping in the evening light off the coast of
Formby, with the wreckage of the Ionic Star in
the background, November 1966.
Left, a rescue bid for a young dolphin, stuck
behind the lock gates at Eastham Lock, 1991.
The baby mammal followed an RSPCA rescue
launch out of the canal and into the River
Mersey after a day-long operation

DRILL WATCH

Members of the
crew of Belfast
Steamship
Company's Ulster
Monarch at lifeboat
drill on arrival in
Liverpool, 1959.
Note the nursing
sister and two
stewards wearing
dickie bows!

The bright sunshine of May 1951 brings crowds in their thousands to the Pier Head, where this picture shows them boarding the New Brighton ferry boat

As the heat wave hit Liverpool in July 1969, office workers flocked to the Pier Head to catch some sun. Even this scene is changed today as the new Leeds and Liverpool Canal extension to Albert Dock has replaced this lawn, but King Edward VII remains on his horse

YACHTIES AND...

Fiddlers Ferry sailing club in June 1968, where the river broadens out into a wide, sweeping bend

DONKEYS

Fun on the beach at New Brighton for three-year-old David Pearson, from Birkenhead, aboard his lilo. Carl Tharme, 9, of Liverpool, preferred a paddle, while others take a donkey ride near the pier, 1961

Men in boaters and women in cotton dresses watch these elegant yachts in a pre-war race off Woodside. Note how only the chancel of Liverpool Cathedral has been built on the centre skyline

An International Garden Festival flotilla led by the yacht Sir Francis Drake makes its way down river from Garston along the Festival Promenade, June 1985

Above, spectators enjoy a band concert in Vale Park, New Brighton, as the ferry Royal Iris sails above the trees. Below, wind-whipped Mersey waves wash the Pier Head walk. There was only railing room in March 1960, when an unusually high tide swept over on to the promenade

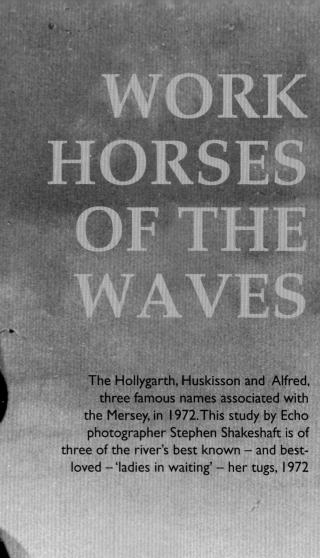

WORK HORSES OF THE WAVES

The Hollygarth, Huskisson and Alfred, three famous names associated with the Mersey, in 1972. This study by Echo photographer Stephen Shakeshaft is of three of the river's best known – and best-loved – 'ladies in waiting' – her tugs, 1972

Fog on the Mersey, 1966, with two Alexandra Towing Company tugs at Princes Landing Stage

QUARTET

Four tugs quadruple-berthed, from left, Alexandra's Formby; and Rea's Throstlegarth, Rosegarth and Applegarth – the latter was sunk in a tragic accident off Birkenhead

The Canadian Pacific tourist class liner Montrose is refloated off a Mersey sandbank in February, 1933. Leading, front left, is CP's own tender tug Bison, with two Alexandra tugs and another CP one at the rear

Above, the distinctive streamlining of Wallasey Corp's 1951 cruise ferry Royal Iris shows as she lies at the landing stage awaiting her passengers. Bottom, passengers enjoy a pleasure cruise on board the first Royal Iris, September 12, 1931

"Royal Iris" on River Cruise

Above, Captain Wilf Peterson finds time for a friendly chat with passengers on board the Royal Iris in 1972. Keeping the engines turning on the Royal Iris in 1966, Chief Engineer Tom Ormerod of Liscard. Bottom, Mersey ferry MV Woodchurch in dock, November 1962

Birkenhead ferry MV Mountwood seen at the George's Stage surrounded by turbulent water during a high wind in September, 1966

Commuters wait at Princes Landing Stage for MV Mountwood, August 1974, which was renamed Royal Iris of the Mersey, in 2002

FLOATING AROUND

Grainworkers, Buckwheat and Coriander – the barges, owned and operated by the Liverpool Grain Storage and Transit Co Ltd, are seen unloading French milling wheat in Brunswick Dock in September 1975. Right, harsh conditions in the frozen Mersey at Seacombe, January 15, 1982

Mersey Docks and Harbour Board's salvage vessel Vigilant with the tanker Constantine in the background, at Tranmere Oil Terminal

UP AND AWAY: ICONS OF THE CITY

PANORAMIC

A view from the Royal Liver Building with, from left, Albion House (ex-White Star Line HQ), Liverpool Cathedral (minus the nave), George's Dock Vent tower, Canning and Salthouse Docks, and Port of Liverpool Building's domes

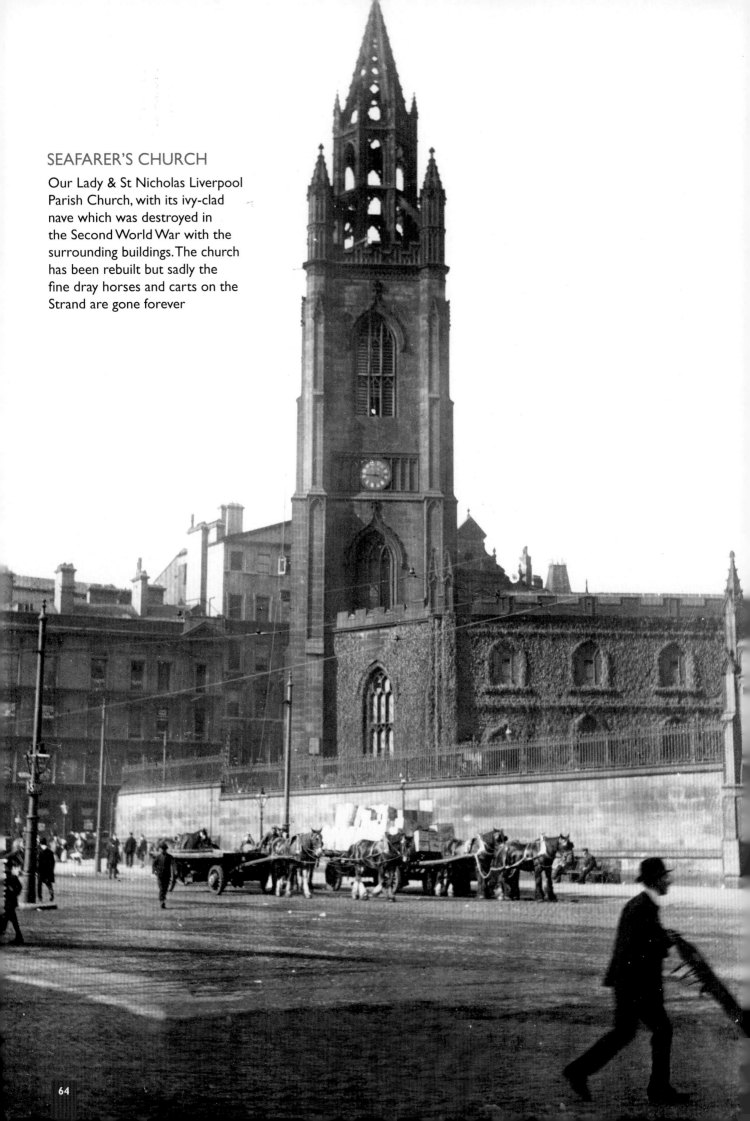

SEAFARER'S CHURCH

Our Lady & St Nicholas Liverpool Parish Church, with its ivy-clad nave which was destroyed in the Second World War with the surrounding buildings. The church has been rebuilt but sadly the fine dray horses and carts on the Strand are gone forever

RARE VIEW
Victoria Tower, Salisbury Dock, and those Clarence Dock 'Three Ugly Sisters' again. Right, a somewhat tired-looking Perch Rock lighthouse at New Brighton and the mouth of the Mersey

A gateman's hut at Canning Half-tide Dock is carefully repositioned during the Albert Dock restoration in the 1980s

OLD AND NEW

This sensational picture of Liverpool Customs House's Strand entrance portico, disgracefully demolished in 1948, reeks of old Liverpool. This February 1935 view shows scaffolding being removed from the new Mersey Tunnel George's Dock Vent, left, and the drays which once thronged the Dock Road. Right, offices of the Mersey Mission to Seamen, James Street, Liverpool, 1959

The 'Ugly Sisters' – the chimneys at Liverpool's Clarence Dock power station, July 1960, and the remains of the Overhead Railway, left

North Wall lighthouse being demolished in 1928. It also housed the 'Bull' foghorn

Engineers, with the aid of the Mersey's 200-foot high Mammoth crane, tugs and massive sea anchors, try to secure the weakened landing stage from a high tide in 1974 – Mammoth lifts free one of the booms from the new landing stage at the Pier Head

UNDER AND OVER

Grummetting and tightening bolts on
the Mersey Tunnel, March 18, 1930

GOING UNDERGROUND

Above, miners on their way to the rock face of the pilot tunnel for the second Mersey Tunnel in 1966. Right, the Mersey Mole emerges through the rock face in 1970. As the revolving cutter sliced its way through the last pieces of sandstone, men watching the operation let out a cheer. Liverpool ECHO photographer Eddie Barford had to jump for his life when heavy lumps of roof rock fell within inches of where he was standing

Mersey Tunnel
December 30, 1929

TICKET TO RIDE

The Overhead Railway Bridge in Liverpool 1955, from James Street. Right, 'the Ovee' is seen in the distance from the floating roadway, June 1953, with, from left, the Titanic Memorial, Our Lady & St Nicholas Church tower and Tower Buildings

UP IN THE CLOUDS

Liverpool Airport with its Mersey River backdrop pictured in November 1988, with a Boeing 707 jet airliner, left – the introduction of which in 1958 doomed ocean liner travel

BRIDGING THE GAP

The new £3m Runcorn - Widnes (later Silver Jubilee) road bridge nears completion on a clear day on October 8, 1961, ready for royal opening by HRH Princess Alexandra, on October 21, with the Britannia Railway Bridge behind and the Transporter Bridge (with cradle seen midway) in front

The tall ship Kathleen & May, built
at Connah's Quay, Deeside, in 1900,
in Liverpool ahead of Mersey River
Festival 2013. Opposite page, two geese
land on East Float Dock, Birkenhead,
alongside the laid-up Mersey ferry MV
Royal Daffodil (ex-Overchurch)

A NEW ERA

By Peter Elson

THE River Mersey's appearance drastically changed for the worse in the early 1970s as traditional shipping disappeared.

Gone were longterm mainstays such as passengers sailings from Princes Landing Stage and the South Docks shipping.

Simultaneously, there was a drastic fall in use of the North Docks and traffic for the Manchester Ship Canal.

Passengers deserted ocean liners for jet airliners (or six hours' travel instead of six days) and one giant container ship replaced six or seven traditional cargo boats.

But in another sense, the trade simply changed into a different and more viable, if less visible form and recently even long distance seabourn passengers have returned to the Pier Head aboard international cruise liners.

The seeds of this started far earlier than many people realise.

Tranmere Oil Terminal was opened in June, 1960, to handle vessels of up to 65,000 tons, and is connected via a 15mile pipeline to the Stanlow Oil Refinery, which can handle 12m tons of cruide oil a year.

While the weekly passenger sailings to North America are no more, ACL – Atlantic Container Lines – which was founded by a

partnership including Cunard Line, has a solid reputation built up since 1969.

Liverpool is at the heart of ACL's linking Europe and North America with a 35-day schedule from Liverpool to Antwerp, Gothenburg, Hamburg, Halifax (NS), New York, Baltimore and Norfolk (Virginia).

Ian Higby, ACL's manager director, said: "We're in Liverpool as it continues to be the right place for our business, closest to the manufacturing heart of the UK."

ACL is building its next generation of super-container ships, the G4 class, with their unique roll-on/roll-off facility to take more and bigger vehicles along with the increased container capacity from 2014.

While these ships are designed to negotiate the Gladstone Lock with their "Gladamax" dimensions, the docks' owner, Peel Ports Mersey, is making a huge investment in a ➤

➤ river berth for the world's biggest container ships for the "Post Panamax" era. This is driven by the widening of the Panama Canal, allowing far bigger container vessels to sail directly from the Far East through the Caribbean and into Europe. These floating behemoths can carry up to 13,500 containers each, which is four times the capacity of current ships.

Called Liverpool 2, the £300m investment now under construction will comprise a 850m long in-river double berth which dispenses with entering the dock system.

The new facility will directly create 500 extra jobs for dock staff, with a possible 4,500 more jobs in the North West. The port currently employs 1,000 and handles 35m tons of cargo a year.

Gary Hodgson, Peel Ports Mersey managing director, said: "There is no doubt that this facility represents a transformational project for the business. It will bring jobs and economic prosperity to Merseyside and the North West."

Liverpool Cruise Terminal has been one of the city's great successes, allowing the biggest cruise liners in the in world to "park in the heart of the city", as

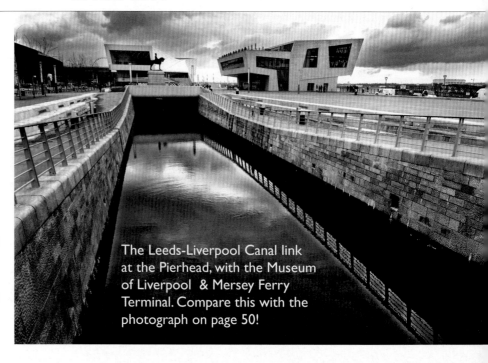

The Leeds-Liverpool Canal link at the Pierhead, with the Museum of Liverpool & Mersey Ferry Terminal. Compare this with the photograph on page 50!

exemplified by the arrival of the Cunard Line's flagship RMS Queen Mary 2.

The terminal was appropriately opened in 2007 by Cunard's previous flagship RMS Queen Elizabeth 2, as the line was founded here and its first sailing was in 1840.

During the terminal's first full season in 2008, there were 13 liner transit calls on round-Britain cruises. This is steadily rising and more than doubled from 15 calls in 2011 to 32 calls in 2012. There are 42 calls in 2013, with 52 calls already booked for 2014. Passenger satisfaction is well ahead of any other UK port destination.

In addition, following a campaign by the Liverpool Post & Echo newspapers, turnaround voyages (ie for passengers to embark and disembark) were revived from the Pier Head in 2012 after a gap of 41 years.

After a modest start with Cruise & Maritime Voyages' small liner MV Ocean Countess, cruises from Liverpool are now being offered on five star-rated ships like Queen Mary 2 and Celebrity Infinity.

This is already re-establishing Liverpool as a major departure point for sea travel, with a new hinterland of visitors stretching from the north Midlands to southern Scotland.

As Liverpool is among that elite group of port cities which are both a cruise tourism destination and a departure port, there is a wealth of new business to be had by combining a city hotel stay with a cruise. An unexpected bonus has been the use of the Cruise Terminal for tall ships visits, special events like the Battle of the Atlantic 70th commemoration, NATO warship gatherings and windfarm, oil and gas support ships.

The latter vessels connect with another Mersey renaissance, that of Cammell Laird shipyard, founded by William Laird in 1828. ➤

MAKING A SPLASH

Clockwise from top: canoe waterpolo under the ECHO Big Wheel in the Albert Dock; swimmers take a Boxing Day plunge into Salthouse Dock; Batala Liverpool bring the sound of samba to On the Waterfront festival; the Beatles Museum at the Pier Head Ferry Terminal; soaking up the sunshine from the roof terrace of Matou restaurant; mechanical spider La Machine draws the crowds in 2008

Much of its recent success is through diversification into wider engineering, including constructing and servicing the Irish Sea windfarm, oil and gas sectors, plus heavy fabrication and civil nuclear power.

It won a £28m Ministry of Defence contract to overhaul the Royal Fleet Auxiliary ships five years ago which has just been renewed. After completing a £44m order for the flight decks of the Royal Navy's new aircraft carrier HMS Queen Elizabeth, it also restarted building complete ships with the construction of two car ferries for Western Ferries on the Clyde.

Taken together, these developments are not so much an exciting new chapter, but an entire volume, in Liverpool and Merseyside's progress, with all of it spun off once again from our exceptional maritime trade.

Liverpool invented the skyscraper and the Royal Liver Building was one of the first in the world to use reinforced concrete. It was the tallest storied building in Europe on completion in 1911.

Together with its two Pier Head companions – the Cunard and Port of Liverpool Buildings – they still speak of the confidence and ambition which was so abundant a century ago and form a symbolic link to the Merseyside renaissance which will extend to the massive Liverpool Waters and Wirral Waters high-rise redevelopment of derelict dockland.

RIVER RENAISSANCE

The newly revived Mersey River Festival in June 2013 was blessed with fine weather, above, as cruise liner Celebrity Infinity forms a backdrop to a Pier Head concert. Right, from top, Alex Elson watches a ferry leave from high on the cruise liner Caribbean Princess; a narrowboat leaving the Leeds-Liverpool canal link, dwarfed by the Crown Princess berthed at the Liverpool Cruise Liner Terminal; Caribbean Princess moored at the Cruise Liner Terminal in 2012

Peel Holdings' £5.5bn Liverpool Waters scheme could start next year after the Government gave it the go-ahead. These artists impressions show how Liverpool's waterfront could be transformed

Right, from top; Tranmere Oil Terminal; Kenny Dalglish officially declares the start of work on container berth Liverpool 2; Irish Ferries' Ulysses in Cammell Laird's dry dock with Birkenhead Priory behind

Two workmen risk the spray on their faces as they enjoy the dramatic outlook on a stormy Mersey, in October, 1958, from the wall of the Huskisson Dock, Liverpool, with, it would appear, a Blue Star cargo-liner in the distance

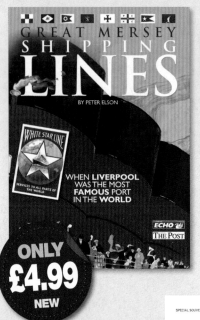
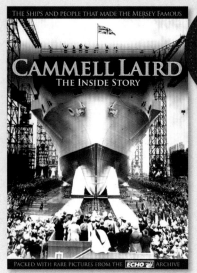
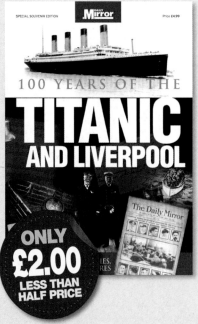